# STAYING In CONTROL

# Staying *in*
# CONTROL

*By*
## ANA M. SILVA

Library of Congress Catalog Number: 00 1-868375

ISBN
Paperback 13: 978-0-9891582-0-6

# *Table of Contents*

Acknowledgements

Prologue

Epilogue

About the Author

# Acknowledgements

*Special Thanks to:*

**Lisa Moon** - Editor

**Eileen Key** - Editor

**Gabriel Gurrola** - Graphic Designer

**Guillermo Velez** - Photographer

**Abigail S. Peurifoy** - Final Details

**Jacqueline Tellez**

**Michelle Cahill**

**Allison Uribe**

**Shauna Lee Priddy**

*Thank you to my family and all my friends for their support.
I would like to dedicate the last two chapters to my children.*

# Prologue

Staying in control when you are in the face of adversity is key to ~~achieve~~ victory. I will share with you what I learned from my many challenges, and what has sustained me during my darkest moments. I discover internal strength to not only survive but also to emerge with new focus and direction. Creating and having a new life with a purpose.

While no one thinks cancer is pleasant, it didn't just make me uncomfortable, it frightened me to think how fast this disease would consume a person's life. I was young, in shape, and enjoyed a healthy diet. I took good care of myself physically. Since there was no history of cancer in my family, I had nothing to worry about.

In 2004 I was feeling strange and disconcerting symptoms. After sending me to the hospital for a CAT scan, my doctor found an aggressive cancer consuming my body. Then, much to my dismay, cancer shattered my peaceful life. Now, I was forced to deal with this monster cancer. The destructive force was within my own body, in my own cells. This intruder could not be shut out.

I felt the deepest conviction that, as simplistic as it sounds, everything was going to turn out just fine. From the beginning, I knew somehow that I was going to survive. Even more, I felt that I needed to write about my difficult time. Once my recovery was complete, I could share what I had overcome to help others.

Right on the heels of the cancer two more traumatic events followed. I discovered that my husband had been having an affair. Two years later while I was still putting my life back together, after the heartbreak and divorce, my closest brother was killed in a car accident. I was barely gathering the pieces after one traumatic event when another would follow. My life made no sense. Doubts, fears, and unanswered questions crowded every waking moment... why was all this happening to me? What purpose could it possibly serve? And how on earth would I make it through this?

A few words describe that period in my life: lost, alone, darkness, pain. Coming to the end of myself, of my very existence.

After trauma, grief, or heartbreak, we come to a crossroads. We can sink in our despair. We can deaden ourselves to pain and live the rest of our lives with detached numbness. Or we can take what seems like the more difficult path: we can move forward. I made a decision to trust God, to consciously maintain a positive attitude, and to believe that the darkness of these awful years had a greater purpose in my life. I entrusted God with my future. Even though I couldn't see it, I knew He could. Now six years later, I have a clear vision for the purpose I want to serve. I work toward it and stay focused. All the pain and confusion of the previous six years have worked in my favor. This has kept me close to God and has helped me push toward my goals.

I am so thankful for one memorable day in November 2010, when I saw a clear picture of my life and my purpose. It was as if the darkness I had been living in was transformed into a beautiful serene life. At last I felt happy, satisfied, and accomplished. I had made it through indescribable pain to experiencing tremendous joy.

I now see that the out-of-control events in my life helped shape me into a better version of myself. They were necessary to forge the positive outlook, drive, and determination that would lead to success. In retrospect, I am in awe of how God restored order to my life. I have so much joy in my heart. Have you seen a child laugh? You start to ask what is so funny, and before the words are out of your mouth, the sweet childish giggles are so contagious that you're laughing too. I feel like that child, I smile and laugh. I better appreciate the joys in my life and the laughter bubbles forth.

I pray that my story will give you hope and courage. Hope for the joy to come in your life. You have a loving God who knows what He is doing. God will care for you with great tenderness. I pray that you find the courage to envision a wonderful future, to lift yourself out of negativity and despair, and to achieve all your dreams.

# CHAPTER 1

# Fighting for my life

I started the year of 2004 filled with fresh hopes and goals. I decided that this would be my year to excel in every area of my life. I relished my role as a mother of two beautiful girls and a baby boy. I was one semester away from accomplishing a lifelong dream of mine: achieving a degree in Interior Design.

A few months later, as I was working on a school project in the middle of the night, I felt a hot spot around my belly button. Alarmed, I rushed to the hospital and the doctor examined the area. I sighed with relief when I was told it was only a torn muscle, nothing worse. I just needed to see my family doctor the next day and get a referral for a surgeon to fix the problem. It was a mundane occurrence, nothing to worry about. The next day my doctor told me she thought I might have a hernia. An appointment was scheduled with a surgeon a few days later.

Dr. Bradshaw was able to fit me into his schedule. As I was lying on the examination table, I was relieved to finally take care of this problem and to move on with my busy life.

I will never forget the surgeon's reaction when he saw the lump around my belly button. "I don't know what this is" he sounded worried. "I've never seen anything like this." Then he started writing on his chart. "I'm going to send you right over to the hospital for a CAT scan and a few other tests so we can see what you have. I do know that it's not a hernia or a torn muscle."

I was calm at the hospital and at ease when I got home after the tests. I had wonderful doctors, and knew someone would figure this out and fix me soon enough. When Dr. Bradshaw called me a few hours later to say he wanted to see me that same day, I still wasn't alarmed. Frankly, I was happy the doctor was working so diligently on my state of being. I was tired of feeling sick so often, and figured that taking care of this hernia, or whatever it was, would get me back to my normal energetic self. I had no idea what the doctor would tell me, but at least progress was being made.

I returned to Dr. Bradshaw's office and sat down in front of his desk. He began, "I'm glad I sent you to get a CAT scan, Ana. I'm afraid I have some bad news." Instantly I felt as if I'd been plunged into a deep, dark hole. I stared at him, with only one overwhelming thought: *Oh no... What do I have??* Dr. Bradshaw continued, "I'm sorry, but you have stage four ovarian cancer, and it doesn't look good at all. The cancer has spread to some of your organs. You have fluid in one of your lungs. That lump around your belly button is fluid." *I'm going to die young... I'm only in my twenties...* "I can't do the surgery, Ana, so I'm going to send you to another specialist."

I could hardly concentrate. The doctor's voice sounded distant. "Do you have any questions?"

Numbly, I shook my head no. I had no words, no questions. My attention couldn't focus on details. In total shock, my mind would only dwell on the same thoughts: *I'm going to die... that's why I was feeling sick all this time... but I saw doctors, no one found this before... and now this is it...* From that moment on, I felt like I walked into a cold, dark tunnel. No light. No exit.

I staggered out of the office, still numb. I never would have guessed that I would be hearing an undeserved death sentence. My life was ending so soon. My kids were so young. So many thoughts flooded my mind... somehow I made it home.

Later that afternoon I heard from the oncologist, Dr. J. White. Due to the critical nature of my situation, we needed to move fast.

At Dr. White's office, he and I sat down to discuss the issues. I scanned his office while I waited. I noticed that he was a runner and a hunter. He entered the room and his first words to me were, "Do you understand how bad your situation is?" I just looked at him, unable to answer. "Do you have kids?" I answered yes, and then he asked me something I will never forget: "Who is going to take care of them?"

Right away I answered, "My mother." I knew that she would care for them, and that my children would need her. My husband Ferr was relatively cold and our relationship was troubled during this time. Dr. White continued asking questions, writing all the while. "This is a very aggressive cancer, Ana. It can consume you in weeks. We'll do the surgery right away."

As Dr. White started to describe the procedure, I worried that even if I survived the surgery, my life would never be the same. I closed my eyes and spoke directly to God. *"I need You to heal me,"* I prayed. *"You know that my girls, and especially my baby boy, need me. I'm not done. I'm still needed here."* Vaguely I heard Dr. White tell me he'd see me in the hospital on Monday. I just kept pleading with God internally. *"I need healing. I need to live a normal life after the surgery. My God you can heal me, I know you can! You're in control now."*

That Friday, as soon as I got home, I called my mother, worried about what to tell her. How much bad news could I deliver without causing her so much worry and grief? I had made a decision. "Mom," I said, "I'm having a minor surgery on Monday." I kept my voice calm and made it sound like it was nothing major. When she asked me why, I said, as lightly as I could manage, "I have a small area of cancer cells, but am going to be fine. The doctor needs to clean some areas to stop it from growing. It really is nothing significant, Mom. Don't worry."

Then I contacted the rest of my family in El Paso. Unfortunately I wasn't able to maintain my casual pretense much longer. My younger sister worked at a local hospital's radiology department, and she did some investigation. When she found out how serious the cancer really was, my secret was out. The whole family was instantly in shock, scared, and anxious for me. My brother Mario took the news hardest of all. He cried like a baby, asking God, "Why Ana? Why her, God?" Mario and I had many things in common and were very close. He, my mother and the rest of my siblings arrived in San Antonio that weekend to be with me the day of the surgery.

I remember vowing to be strong for my family's sake. I acted as if the surgery and the cancer were nothing. But I could feel their fear and worry. They were scared that this might be the last time they would see me alive.

On Monday morning, I was prepared to go to the hospital. I told my older sister, who is like a second mother to me, "I want to do your make-up and your hair today," and she agreed. I smiled at her. I put make-up on her pretty face and curled her long black hair. It was my small way of maintaining a bit of normalcy. I just wanted to cheer everyone up as if there was nothing to worry about. She looked so beautiful, but I could see sadness in her dark brown eyes. I laughed, "I am going to be fine, Sis!" as I gave her a big hug. We walked downstairs, ready to go to the hospital at last.

In the living room, one of my pastors from El Paso and his wife were waiting for me. They had driven the eight hours to support me and pray for my healing. As we prayed together, my one thought was for a miracle. *I'm going to go through surgery today, God. I need You to be my surgeon. I'll be waiting for Your miracle. I put my kids and myself in Your hands. I need Your help, my family needs Your help to be strong. I give You control of this pain, Lord.*

I faltered, but ceded control to God again, knowing I had to. In order to relax and maintain the calmness I needed to take the next step. I took a deep breath. *Thank You for all that You do, and thank You for my miracle, Lord.* I decided, despite my prognosis, to live in faith and hold onto hope for my life. Sometimes you have no choice but to believe the impossible and live by faith.

*Now faith is the substance of things hoped for, the evidence of things not seen. Hebrews 11:1*

When I arrived at the hospital, I saw many dear and wonderful people waiting there for me. It touched me so much to see my friends and church family come in the wee hours of the morning. I tried not to think that this might be the last time I would see these people who were so dear to me. I could tell they were trying not to think the same thing. I saw many sad faces trying to be brave, but sometimes it felt like they were giving me their last hug. I embraced everyone and told them over and over, "I'm going to be fine! I will be back." I smiled as I walked away. I knew they were worried, but I had turned it all over to God. I was calm enough to move forward.

Three specialists, including Dr. Bradshaw, were preparing for the long, delicate surgery. I held my composure while the nurses prepared me, but there was an undercurrent of anxiety and a whole host of emotions that I was feeling. Yet, I didn't lose my faith in the ultimate Healer. I knew that my trust was in the right place, in God. I was expecting a miracle.

Dr. Bradshaw came into the room with a smile. "Ana, I'm leaving now. I'm not going to take your spleen out. I think you will be fine. You really don't need me here anymore," he smiled. He told me Dr. White would call if he thought he needed to see me and then said cheerfully, "See you Christmas shopping!"

Since it was still September, I knew he was just trying to make me laugh. I just smiled back and said, "Thank you so much for everything." I still had two surgeons waiting for me in the operating room. The nurse came for me and moved me to a different room. It was a large area with three other patients. I heard a lady crying, and with my eyes closed, asked God to have mercy and bring healing to her body. I knew that my miracle was on its way. Dr. White walked into the room at that moment and asked me what was wrong. "Nothing," I said, "I was praying for the lady next to me, she is in pain." He put his head down and I could almost read his thoughts: you are really bad off yourself, and praying for someone also. He said to me, "Okay we're ready for you. See you in the operating room." And with his head down, he stepped outside.

When I was wheeled into the operating room I remember looking around with such courage, thinking to myself, "I will experience a miracle in this room." The surgery took several hours, but for me it was over before I knew it. I woke up slowly and remember hearing a voice say, "She looks good." I just smiled with my eyes closed as the nurses took me to the recovery room. All that was left to do was rest and recover.

The next day Dr. White came to check on me. His words were fresh life: "Everything went well. We thought it was ovarian cancer, but it's not. Honestly, I have never seen anything like it. And you still have your beautiful belly button,

I didn't remove it." I gave him a big smile. Then he went on, "But it is still a type of cancer, and as soon as you get out of the hospital you need to see an oncologist. I will send you to one who is close, so you can start chemotherapy to kill off any remaining problematic cells. I cleaned everything well, and you should be fine.

Dr. Wilks will take it from here." I knew God had heard my prayer and I witnessed a miracle, but apparently it was not yet complete. The other part of my miracle was on its way. Dr. Wilks' office called my house a few days after I left the hospital to let me know they were ready to see me. At that point I was completely weak, trying to heal from the surgery, under strong medication for pain. The result was that everything felt like a bad dream... only it was all too real. Ferr took me to my appointment a few days after the surgery.

During this time, he was emotionally distant from me. In addition to trying to recover, I had to deal with the sense of being alone and disappointed. As I was in the room waiting for the doctor, I was feeling so tired and frail. I couldn't hold myself up. I was struggling to stay alert and just wanted to stay in bed.

At last she walked in. I was lying on the examination table, cold, hurting, and feeble. Dr. Wilks started to explain the mystery of what I had. "The cancer you have is called

Burkett's lymphoma. It is common in men but not in women. The cancer usually happens to people younger than thirty and it is believed that it can be triggered by a chemical reaction..." I was just listening with the portion of my brain that wasn't consumed with pain and could focus, and thinking to myself, *"This is torture, God."* Then she started telling me about the treatments. It was as if another heavy load had been dropped on me, on top of the heavy load I was already struggling with. "I consulted with the other doctors about your cancer, and we put a treatment together specifically for you. I'll need to see you five days a week, and it will take about eight months. Then hopefully this will be the end of the treatment." She gave my hand a squeeze and stepped outside the room.

I closed my eyes as tears came down my cheeks. I started to pray. *"This is too much for me, God. I don't think I can handle all this. I can't do it. It's too much. I don't have the physical or mental strength."*

A few minutes later the doctor returned. "Okay," she said, "I changed the treatment. I will see you three times a week, and it will be for six months instead of eight."

It was almost as if Dr. Wilks had heard me talking to God. At that moment I vowed that, when I got better, I would write about my experience. Everything that was happening to me was unreal, yet I knew God was hearing my prayers and He was in control of this awful mess.

Soon enough I started my first round of treatment and a new nightmare began. The first chemotherapy treatment did not go well. It left me so sick I felt like a shell of my former self. Since my memory of that time is hazy, I looked back at the notes my sister-in-law Sylvia wrote in her dairy. I couldn't keep anything in my stomach and I was very weak. Even if I could've kept food down, I had no appetite and was very sleepy all the time.

My weight dropped to ninety-six pounds very quickly. At the treatment appointments I would look around at other patients and felt like I was far worse than they were. My mother left her job and moved in with me during that time to care for me. I couldn't do much more than lie down, so my life changed from that of an active person to that of someone who couldn't get out of her own bed. I used to run three miles a day, work out nearly every day, and eat healthy before all this happened. Now I couldn't do one thing to contribute to my own recovery.

One day on my way to the doctor's office, I saw people running on the trail I used to run before I got sick. With painful mixed emotions and tears in my eyes, I looked out the window wanting to run again someday. I was so weak it seemed impossible to even hope for. I remember how excited I was when the doctor told me, "I'm going to give you some medicine that'll help with your energy level." I was so happy to feel slightly back to normal. But even with the medication, I couldn't do much. When I got home the weakness took over again, and all I could do was sleep.

Although I was in the same house that my children were in, I was hardly able to interact with them and that was hard for me to accept. Soon after I began treatment, my hair started to fall out. Now that the illness was apparent, I wanted to ensure that my daughters wouldn't be scared. So I asked my nephew Adam to shave my head, but I wanted my girls to be present and be part of the whole transformation. I made it look like I did it by choice, not because I had to. My beautiful long hair was gone along with the healthy glow on my face.

I became a person that the cancer created. A person I would be afraid of every time I saw myself in the mirror. My identity, my self-image was gone, and the resulting instability that I felt was very frightening. The beautiful girl that God created was no longer the same. Yet somehow, while struggling to keep my spirits up for my children's sake, and trying to not inconvenience Ferr (and drive him further away from me), I had to find beauty in all that remained, and rebuild my foundation by finding the beauty within.

No hair, and a sickly yellow tone on my face. This was the outside, but inside my soul and spirit I began to grow strong. My face and body were hard to look at every day, and I had no idea when this painful journey would end. It took all my inner resolve to live one day at a time, keeping faith, and trusting God.

As trivial as it felt at times, talking to family about how hard things were for me to be without my hair helped. Once, as I was sharing with my brother-in-law Saul, he said to me, "I completely understand how you feel." I looked at him in confusion. He continued with his thought, "Ana, you're going to get your hair back some day. Look at me. I'm not." He was bald. We looked at each other seriously. Then he smiled. I couldn't stop laughing. It took that moment of perspective to give me a good day out of all those bad days in my life. In your troubles, find the comical side of it and laugh about it. It's good medicine for your soul, and can help you through the worst moments. Even in the dark days of my life, I would find something positive to hang on to and carry me through.

One day after having been sick for so long, my eight-year-old daughter Kim came and stood by the door of my room. I saw her and weakly said, "Come in, pretty girl." I was very sick in bed. She came to me, and I was determined to act like everything was normal. "How was your day at school?" She said, "Good," with a sad face and watery eyes. I put my arm around her. "Why are you sad?"

"Because you've been sick too long, Mommy." I hugged her, wanting to cry, but made myself strong.

"This is just for a little bit, okay? I'm going to be well soon, you'll see."

Little Kim cried. I could see she was trying bravely not to. "Okay, Mommy. I just don't like to see you sick like this."

"I know, pretty, but I am just a little sick, that's all, okay? Now, I don't like to see you sad, give me a smile." She did, but it was a sad smile, with tears in her little eyes. As she walked out of the room I started weeping.

Everything was out of my control. It hurt me so much to see Kim cry, telling me in her own way that she needed and missed me. I was losing time with my children, along with everything else. How could this be possible?

As the treatments of chemotherapy progressed I started to show physical side effects. First, I got blisters both inside and outside my mouth. I couldn't swallow my own saliva, which was very painful. My vision would often blur. I was utterly at the mercy of my body's condition. At times I thought that God had forgotten about me, or worse, abandoned me. I prayed all the time but only felt worse with each passing day.

*1- 07.03.0217*

Many times I was transported to the hospital due to high fever, low platelets, not enough white blood cells, or low red blood cells. I walked a very thin line between life and death during treatment. Still, I clung to hope with what little energy I had. God had promised me a victory and I was waiting for it. I often told God, "My mission isn't over. I have my children and they need me. Have mercy, Lord. I need You." I spent many hours listening to gospel music to help calm me during my worst moments.

**I found that gospel music lifted my spirits and filled me with hope. Like laughter, music is good for the soul. We can't always control what comes our way, but we have total control of our soul. We can use that inner strength to fight for survival if we need to.**

Happier moments would eventually follow the horrible ones. One night, when everyone was asleep, I got up from my bed, needing to walk around for a bit. I was having a bad night. Wanting to see my eleven-month old baby boy Max, I walked to the staircase. I looked up and knew that there was no way I had the strength to make the climb. I returned to my bed in tears. I told God I was tired of fighting, that I just wanted a break from everything. If it was truly my time, I was ready. I knew that He would take care of my daughters and my baby boy. Doctors, hospitals, and bed rest consumed my life.

My body was failing me. Without an appetite or the ability to hold down any food, I was incapable of regaining any strength. The emotional and physical burden weighed heavily on me. I felt useless in this world. I cried myself to sleep. Unfortunately, there would be many more nights like this to follow.

The next morning, my mother woke me with an enthusiastic, "Time for breakfast!" I opened my eyes and said to myself in disbelief, "I am still here. Thank you God for another day." Immediately I felt less weak. Slowly, as the days passed, I grew stronger, bit-by-bit. Finally I felt well enough to climb the staircase. *"Wow, I can do this!"* I had surprised myself and I was delighted. I went straight to Max's room, so very excited about this milestone. As I walked into his room I saw my Mom playing with my son. My mother saw me and asked in surprise, "You came up here by yourself?" I told her with a huge smile, "I feel better, Mom!" This tiny bit of improvement felt wonderful!

It had been so long since I'd had the pleasure of being a "mom". I played with my son until I was exhausted. I didn't want to leave him. Before I knew it, it was time for me to get some rest.

Despite my lack of appetite, I occasionally craved certain foods, particularly a certain ice cream that was made in Mexico. During a phone conversation with my brother, Mario, I had mentioned it. He drove eight hours just to bring me a cooler full of ice cream. He always made me feel like a princess. I enjoyed its familiar deliciousness while I laid my head on his shoulder. Those were moments I will never forget, along with the outpouring love.

There were many phone calls and cards from people I didn't know. Yet I knew that God allowed them to hear about my situation so that they would lift me up, and they did. Those angels will never know how much of a blessing they were.

On good days, I would pretend everything was normal again. That's how I survived. As a kid, I remember using my imagination to pretend that I was in magical places. I did the same during this time by imagining that I was healthy and pretending the illness I had didn't exist.

**God gave you an imagination use it when you need it! Imagination isn't only for children. Imagination is a wonderful tool that can carry you through difficult moments in your life. It'll help you make the best out of unpleasant life events you may find yourself in.**

Cancer taught me to always make the best out of everything. I learned that I could overcome whatever comes my way. God has equipped me to be a survivor here on earth. I learned to see each temporary setback as merely one important victory. When I lost my hair, I bought a purple wig and had fun with it. I enjoyed the glow the purple hue gave my skin.

When my weight fell, I was not pretty to look at. It was uncomfortable, even to sit down. I was so skinny; it felt like my bones were piercing my muscles. Even though I was slim before, I now swam in my clothes. My solution was to buy new clothes - it was my favorite thing to do. I went with my niece Victoria, taking small breaks as we shopped. I tired easily, but I was so happy to feel active again.

I had fun layering my clothes and creating different looks. I had never been this thin before, so it was time to have fun. Playing with fashion and color lifted my spirit. When you look good, you feel good. I was painfully aware of my slow progress and dressing up made me feel like a healthy person again. By simply using the power I had to improve my situation and turning a negative into a positive experience. **I would write positive notes, stick them on the mirror, and read them to myself throughout the day. Such a simple thing, yet it made me feel stronger as each day passed**.

The bad days weren't over – there were many more to come. But I used my good days to prepare my mind and body for the bad days.

After my first round of chemotherapy, I was glad it was over. Still I had two phases to go and I was afraid because the first round was miserable. Believe me, I wanted to run away from my second and third treatment phases, but I had to face them. I was willing to face the reality and fight the entire way through. I refused to allow worry and fear to take over my mind.

**The only way to conquer my fear was to stay in the moment and to face each individual obstacle. To let go of what has passed and not torture myself about what may happen. None of us know what will come and the past is gone. I had to surrender each day, each moment to God.**

During the second and third phases of the nearly yearlong treatment, I experienced the same debilitating symptoms and my body showed the same awful side effects. Each time I started chemo, they were poisoning my body all over again. But I knew what would get me going again, thanks to paying close attention to my body during my first treatment. One particular day I thought that was the end of me. My sister-in-law Sylvia called the doctor for me and I went in for fluids. I would feel so much better after I received fluids to help with the dehydration. I called it going in for my happy juice. I'd practically crawl into the doctor's office with no energy, feeling like I was dying, but after my "happy juice" I felt like new again.

At long last, the treatments were over. It was now time to take a PET (Positron Emission Tomography) scan to see if the treatment worked. I stayed positive but was still nervous to find out the results. I had faith that I would witness my miracle. I refused to allow doubt to enter my mind. This was a valuable lesson for me. **When you envision yourself closer to victory and stand in faith mentally, it gives you mental stability, which is vital.** I believed with all my heart and stayed positive.

I saw Dr. Wilks a few days later to learn the results of the PET scan. I was nervous as I waited to hear if the treatment had worked. Over and over I told God, *"I know this is the end of my treatment. Thank you Lord, for all that You did in my life. Thank You for the wonderful doctors You put in my path to take care of me. Thank You for all the days You've given me."* Then Dr. Wilks walked in the room. She gave me a warm hug and said, "Everything looks good now. The treatment we designed for you seems to have done its job. We're all done!"

Finally, I was hearing what I wanted to hear, what I'd been praying for with all the fervency and faith that I had. I hugged her with such joy, and thanked her for all she had done for me. It was all over! I could enjoy life again! **It was time to celebrate life, to celebrate this incredible gift from God. I truly felt like I had been reborn.**

I left Dr. Wilks' office thinking, *"I just witnessed a miracle, and it was in my life,"* I smiled, and thought, *miracles do happen.* **If you believe whole-heartedly you will receive the wonders God has in store for you.**

## *What I Learned, and What Kept Me Going*

Even though I never knew what the future would bring, I knew God was in control. I belong to Him, and He created me with a purpose. He created my body and He had the power to restore my health. **There is always a reason and purpose for everything we face in life. We might not know it at the time, but at the end we know that it had its good purpose. Some events in our lives can be painful and extreme, but it is a process we must go through to make us more beautiful. What is uncomfortable compels us to move to a different place. Beginnings should be welcomed. It's an opportunity to take each day, each situation to improve.**

Many times I felt like I was dying, I couldn't breath and I felt like my body was failing me. During my sleep I had battled for my life. My kids gave me the courage to stay alive and keep fighting. It is important to know what you want and where you are going. Stay strong. **We were created to survive. Make the best of the worst, and remind ourselves that something good always comes from the bad.** Always have a positive attitude toward all the unpleasant events in life.

Face life with a big smile, use all the power you have in you to make it happen. Laugh often, even when things are not so great. Laughter makes the bumpy ride a lot more bearable. Utilize all that you have, all your inner strength, to get to where you want to be.

God is always by your side, even when you feel that He is not there.

I felted like God left me alone in my struggles. I cried out in fear. I used what strength I had left in my soul to create peace of mind. It was very easy to stop believing in God but I choose not to. He was my foundation and I couldn't move from it. God is there for you all the time. Have faith and believe that He is with you.

**Faith is to believe in something you cannot see. The result of faith is to see what you believed in. Faith leads to feeling more secure, confident, and fulfilled. With faith you always make things happen. Faith gives you the courage, the confidence to move on and approach life with a positive attitude.**

## God Puts the Right People in Your Path

I prayed for the best doctor in San Antonio and God answered my prayer through the efforts of my dear friend Tristi. God had put Tristi in my path, and she is a wonderful doctor herself. When I told her about my situation, she gave me a concerned look and then picked up the phone to make sure I was going to get the best surgeon in town. After she talked to some of her colleagues, Tristi reassured me, "You're going to be in good hands. The doctor doing the surgery is one of the best in town. And as for the surgery, you will be able to live a full, normal life afterwards as well."

Then Tristi prayed for me and I felt calm. Hearing her kind words made me feel untroubled. My sweet friend was there in the waiting room the day of the surgery and she stayed the entire day. She was there for me the entire six months of my chemotherapy. Some nights I would call her in the middle of the night when I was feeling sick and didn't know how I could possibly make it through till morning. Tristi would answer my phone calls and tell me what to do to get through the night, and sure enough, I would feel better. She was always right. I will forever be grateful for all that she did for me.

I believe that every person that crosses your path is there for a reason. People come into your life at the right time. I was blessed and surrounded by incredible people. Some of them are no longer part of my life, but they played an important role then. They were a blessing and left me with a lovely memory and a heart filled with gratitude. I am still here because of their contribution. God is an awesome God. He will always provide for you every day, according to your needs, without a doubt.

## *Never Stop Believing*

Being hit with such a traumatic situation took a great deal of time, as well as blood, sweat, and tears to overcome. There are always unpleasant side effects. But with time, everything passes. Time is the only thing that can heal you completely. Now I'm better than I was before, both physically and mentally. I am stronger in all areas of my life. I saw, felt and experienced for myself a miracle that changed me forever.

When 2005 came, I asked God for an excellent year, filled with health, peace, and joy. I received that great year, a year of healing. My body was getting stronger day-by-day, and I was growing stronger mentally as well. My hair started to grow back, and thankfully, it was exactly the same as before treatment. After chemotherapy, hair may grow back a different color or texture, but I had prayed that my hair remain the same as before − straight and light brown. Well it happened just as I asked, I saw it as a special gift from God. To me, hair is a woman's crowning glory and it had been very important for me to feel like my own self again. The glow on my face returned − slowly, but steadily. It took time to recover from the strong treatments of chemo.

During the summer of 2005, I went to New York City with my family and getting away helped me recover mentally. Leaving everything behind for a few days was amazing and renewing. It was time for a new chapter and a new season in my life with my beautiful family.

Experiencing cancer was extremely difficult, but it contributed to making me a better person. Now I understand what it means to be severely sick. Having hit rock bottom, I want to share my miracle with you. I believe in God's power and His mercy, and learned to depend on Him one hundred percent.

**The power we have to make things happen is unbelievable. You learn what you have and what you are made of in the difficult times of your life. We are here on earth to survive and to do well for ourselves. We have what it takes to be successful, overcome anything in life, and always be victorious if we trust in God.**

I used everything that God equipped me with: staying positive and always trusting in God even when I felt alone in my misery. It was a walk by faith. It went against everything I was hearing and feeling at that time, but I allowed God to take total control of my life. Now I know I did the right thing. He saw a bright future that I couldn't see then, but now I'm living it and love it .

God took care of me in my difficult moments, using great people and wonderful doctors. I could see God's hand at work during that time. At times there was no other explanation for something I'd received or experienced, but to say that it was God. He was showing me that my prayers were heard. I could feel at peace because I knew I was in good hands – in God's hands.

Now I live life  with gratitude and that experience made me stronger. The greatest lesson for me is that I found the true meaning of life. I'm still here on earth because my mission is not over, but I know that heaven is my destination.

*Thank You, Lord, for the life lessons.* I have so much joy and feel accomplished due to those experiences.

## *Strength During Difficult Times*

Biblical stories that helped me were the stories of Job and of David facing the giant. I highly recommend you read these great stories if you haven't heard about them yet. Very inspiring. (Job 1-42) ( 1 Samuel 17)

*Hebrews 13:8 reads;*
*"God is the same yesterday, today, and forever."*

If God healed Job and many other people in biblical times, I know He can heal me too. David faced the giant and won the battle. I had the same God and I was going to defeat the giant I was facing.

*Philippians 4:13 reads;*
*"I can do all things through Christ who strengthens me."*

I would repeat this bible verse to myself whenever I felt that I couldn't handle a situation any more, when I was anxiously waiting for test results or times I went to the hospital. I remained calm because I knew God was with me at all times.

*Psalm 46:10*
*"Keep calm and know that I am God."*

I had to remind myself of this bible verse many, many times during treatment.

Everything is possible. It says in Matthew 19:26- *Jesus looked at them and said, "With man this is impossible, but with God all things are possible."*

I believed, achieved, and I know you can do the same. I believed in the impossible. I am a witness of God's power and miracles because I am one. God bless you as you trust and believe in Him. He is the Doctor of doctors, and your Healer. God is still making miracles and can make one in your life today.

# CHAPTER 2

# In Love and Heartbroken

I fell in love at the tender age of fourteen. Like most girls, I had dreamed of finding the "perfect" boy. One day, I met mine. Ferr was a skinny sixteen-year-old with intelligence, whose dark, curly hair contrasted beautifully against his pale skin and in my mind he was the perfect boy for me. I attended church often and would look for him each Sunday. Whenever we made eye contact, I was ecstatic. In a few months, my girlish dream came true and we became boyfriend and girlfriend.

Ferr was popular and greatly admired by the youth at the church for the gift he had of teaching. I admired him. After a blissful two years of dating, he needed to move to Killeen, Texas to work for his father. We decided to continue the relationship despite the distance. Ferr would visit me every weekend. He sent cards and letters daily. We spoke on the phone for hours and during one conversation, Ferr said quietly,

"I want you to marry me. I will talk to your mom, and then you can come with me to Killeen."

"Yes," I cried, "I miss you so much! But what if my mom says no?" I was only sixteen.

"I will still bring you with me," insisted Ferr. "We can ask for permission to go to lunch and then I will bring you away with me. We can call and tell your mom when we get to Killeen." In our young minds, this was a reasonable Plan B.

My beautiful prince Ferr, only eighteen years old, arrived at my house one weekend with a wedding ring: to get married right away. Excited and nervous, I was worried about getting my mother's blessing. I found her in the living room. "Ferr wants to talk to you, Mom."

"With me?"

"Yes, Mom," as I looked away, holding my hand to hide the ring. Sitting down with Ferr, Mom said, "Okay... what do you need to tell me?"

Taking a deep breath, Ferr began, resolutely describing how difficult it was to be away from me. "I have talked to Ana," he said, "and we want to be together. I have the ring... can you give me permission to marry her?"

My mother had tears in her eyes as she looked at us. "You are both so young... too young. But I know that with or without my permission, you are going to get married. It is better that I give you my permission and my blessing." Ferr and I looked at each other, overjoyed, with huge smiles on our faces. Soon after, we had a small ceremony and moved away. I was sixteen and married. I eagerly left my mother and family behind to become part of a new family. All I wanted was to be with Ferr, my prince.

We moved to a different city the day after the wedding. I was a fresh young housewife. Though my days were long and I missed my family terribly, I never questioned or regretted marrying so young. Being with the love of my life made me happy. Finances were tight at times and we needed to work hard and make sacrifices in order to succeed. Having seen my mother strive to accomplish many personal goals in her life, I was willing to take full responsibility for my decision.

I was pregnant by the following year and gave birth to my baby girl, Natali. Two years later, I was delighted to have another baby girl, Kimberli. I was happy with the course my life had taken and enjoyed the responsibility of motherhood. Traveling with two babies was certainly challenging and so was living in different cities for months at a time, away from my family. But that was the nature of my husband's working life and we had to go with him. Once the girls were school-aged, we could no longer travel with Ferr, so I stayed in El Paso, Texas while my husband took many out-of-town trips for work. We still had a wonderful relationship and I missed him greatly whenever work took him away.

I remember Ferr's family doubting me because I married and had my babies so young. I always tried to prove them wrong, to show them that I could do it. Besides being a devoted wife and mother, I wanted to grow as an individual. I enrolled in the university to study Fashion and Interior Design, following in my mother and grandmother's footsteps. Meanwhile, my husband's company began to expand. After nine years of marriage, we moved from El Paso to San Antonio, an eight-hour drive away. Finally all of our hard work had paid off. We were ready for a change in our lives and San Antonio was a great step. I had no family in San Antonio, and the move was painful and lonely for me, but I made the best of it. We had moved in order to have a better life, to expand the family business in a larger city. My babies were growing up and I was close to finishing one degree.

I cared for our precious girls and continued with my education. I had always wanted a baby boy and God was good to me. I received my heart's desire and gave birth to a beautiful baby boy named Max.

I had three beautiful children. I was only in my twenties, but I had everything I wanted in life and I was thankful. Yet I had one growing concern: Ferr was getting extremely busy with work. Furthermore, he didn't want me to continue my studies. In his mind I had everything I needed. While that was true, I wanted to prepare myself professionally in case something happened to Ferr. I always worried about what I would do with three children and no career, should I find myself in need. As any responsible mother would, I wanted to be able to provide for my children.

I had watched my own mother struggle with seven children. She had moved to the United States from Mexico for a better life and she always told us to continue our education and have a career, so that we wouldn't have to work as hard as she had. My mother had to sacrifice so many things for my six siblings and me. Her encouragement and example were a large part of why I pushed myself to complete my degree. I took her advice seriously and I wanted to make her proud.

When I was close to graduating from the university, I started seeing some disturbing changes in our marriage. Ferr was increasingly distant, even when I was pregnant with Max. I would ask him, "Why are you different with me?" He would stay quiet and gave me no answer. Secretly I felt that he didn't want us to have another child, but I had no clue about his unhappiness. I knew that things were not as they should be. We were growing apart but I could do nothing. We still attended church regularly and I thought that so long as we went to church faithfully, things should be fine. The thought of him having an affair did cross my mind. After all, he was always "working." I began to see so much evidence, and I would ask him about items I found in his car, but Ferr insisted his brother had done it as a joke on him. I wasn't fully satisfied. I felt I had no choice but to believe him. We had very little communication. Ferr worked long hours, leaving really early in the morning and coming home late at night. That was not the relationship we had enjoyed before. The kids wouldn't see their father for days. They were sleeping when he left for work in the morning, and back in bed when he came home. Needless to say, I was unhappy and frustrated.

Things went from bad to worse. I continued with my schooling, taking advantage of the time when my own girls were in school. Ferr traveled on business trips more and more. The business trips were very stressful for me. I would call his phone but there would be no answer. He would say his phone had died. One day he finally told me, "Don't call me on the phone-just text me. Look," he added to reassure me, "everyone is doing that now." The distance could hardly grow any bigger.

Many times the thought of divorce went through my mind, but I would remind myself that I had made a promise and I was going to keep it. I was determined to do "the right thing", regardless of whatever emptiness or hardship I was suffering. Plus I truly believed that divorce would ruin my children's lives. Everything has consequences, I knew… and I wasn't about to make others suffer the consequences of my own selfish choices. I was still in love with Ferr. I had married him for better or for worse, and I wanted my children to grow up with their father. Whatever it took to save the marriage, I would do it.

We started counseling. From the beginning it was pointless. Whenever the counselor asked Ferr questions, Ferr would dodge them or answer dishonestly. I was told I just needed to be more patient with Ferr's work schedule. My intuition that something was very wrong was dismissed by the counselor and only drew scorn from Ferr. "Nothing is wrong here, Ana… you're crazy… you're seeing things… you're making things up," I was repeatedly told. We left each session with nothing resolved and me feeling worse than before. We took a break from counseling for a year, and then began again with a therapist named Robin.

While we made some progress with Robin, the results only seemed to be temporary. We saw her for three years. After a while, the constant drain of emotional energy took its toll. Honestly, I got tired of the counseling treadmill. We had to go every week, yet I felt that after three years, we should have accomplished our goals. The occasional improvements in Ferr's communication with me seemed insincere, as if he was only completing a homework assignment. We put in another year of counseling sessions but then stopped entirely and the state of our marriage reverted to its status of "stalemate."

As it happened, I didn't live in this state of cold isolation for much longer. One morning, as I was getting ready for my daily run, I spotted a DVD in an envelope on the doorstep. I handed it to my thirteen-year-old daughter, "Here, mama, your cousin must've sent this for you." When I came back in the front door, breathless from my run, Natali gave me an odd look and said, "Mom... It's not from my cousin. I don't know who gave this to us."

Immediately, my internal alarm bells went off. Worried sick, though I didn't know why, I called Ferr and asked about the DVD. Ferr reacted with impressive drama. He said he would be home right away; I wasn't to open the DVD or even touch it. He claimed the DVD had some sort of biological virus. I warned Natali and silently prayed that nothing bad would happen to us. Both my daughter and I had handled the envelope.

Ferr arrived and insisted that the DVD was tainted. All of his family received one, he said. He reassured me that they were all fine, but the envelope and its contents needed to be destroyed. I stared at him in disbelief. Who would do such a thing? I asked him. We don't have enemies... "Our business is doing great," Ferr shrugged. "In business, you make enemies." At my insistence, Ferr reluctantly agreed to fill out a police report and he headed back to the office.

Left home, still in shock, I was unsettled. *A virus-infected DVD, left on our doorstep by business enemies?* Wanting to believe Ferr, but unable to accept such a far-fetched explanation, I called him back and asked if he'd filed the police report. Ferr reassured me that he had. Taking a deep breath to fill myself with courage, I asked him, "Can you give me the report number? I need to know what that DVD had in it." Ferr's evasiveness confirmed my worst fears. I got in my car and headed straight to his work. As I walked into his office I happened to look down, and there in a trash can by the door was the mysterious DVD, broken in pieces. At that point I knew. Something had been on that DVD that he didn't want me to see. Ferr and I started a heated argument. "You lied to me! What is going on?" I cried, but Ferr's attempts at an explanation made no sense.

"My brother did this," he told me, "He's trying to destroy our marriage, Ana. Are you going to let him do this?" I stared at Ferr in utter disbelief. If I hadn't been so scared about the state of my marriage and my family, I would have been offended that he could think I was so naive. Without having received one answer that made sense, I drove home in a fog of anxiety, anger, and fear.

Late that night, while Ferr was still at work, I was awakened by a phone call. A man's voice I'd never heard said, "I'm sorry things had to happen this way," and hung up. Now I was truly frightened. I tried calling back, but the phone number was blocked. To this day I have no explanation for who called that night, but I vividly remember how I felt. In an instant I had been taken from my unhappy but somewhat ordinary life and dropped into a war zone. I was being assaulted by unknown enemies. At the time, Ferr was working on a project that required him to be on site until three or four in the morning. I spent sleepless nights wondering what had been on that mysterious DVD and who could possibly want to hurt my family.

The next morning, exhausted and numb, I called one of my sisters-in-law to ask if she had received a strange DVD. My body was shaking from all the mixed emotions I was feeling, but inside I stayed in control. I closed my eyes when she paused and said, "Yes, ask Ferr, but if he doesn't tell you, then come and watch the DVD here. I'll show you, and you can keep it. It belongs to you, Ana."

Convinced at last that he had been unfaithful, I called Ferr and insisted he tell the truth for once. My sister-in-law had a copy of the DVD, and I was headed to her house to see it.

He insisted that I meet him at home instead and I agreed. When he arrived, he was clearly nervous and had the air of someone who has been rehearsing a speech. "Look," Ferr began, arms crossed in front of him. "I'm in that DVD, with a friend. But she's only a friend. Nothing more."

I asked questions as they came to me and he fed me lie after lie. The ugly truth was becoming clear at last: Ferr was not the person I thought he was. The pain of this discovery as it sank in over the next days and weeks was hard to describe. Ferr was a stranger to me, living a life based upon lies. My entire family, the core of my life, was based on lies. I thought I knew who my husband truly was, but I didn't. At that moment, faced with a man who couldn't answer the simplest of questions, who clearly had been cheating on me for God knows how long, the foundational truths of my life dissolved into a shapeless, unnerving void. In an instant, I had nothing.

I looked at Ferr and saw him clearly as the person he really was: a total stranger. I walked out the door and went to my sister-in-law's house. Once I got there, I gathered the strength to watch the DVD. All the evidence that I had known existed for five years was on that disc. *She's only a friend. Nothing more,* I heard Ferr's voice echo in my head and I couldn't believe he had the audacity to deny anything was happening. Once again, I drove home and faced the man

I thought I knew. "Give me her phone number. I want to talk to her myself." Surprisingly, Ferr complied.

The woman was calm, almost professional on the phone. She insisted she hadn't known Ferr was married and said that they had met at a gas station. Ferr had tried to feed me the same line about meeting at a gas station and I knew it was a lie. It turned out that the woman knew everything about Ferr – that he was married, our children's names, about his work. The woman's brother, in fact, was working for our company – Ferr had hired him as a favor to his lover. She probably knew him better than I did.

After that dreadful phone call, I turned to Ferr. We had been talking in our bathroom, so that the kids couldn't hear. "What do you want to do now?" I asked him.

Ferr didn't answer. He leaned against the wall with his head down, arms crossed defensively in front of him. He'd been doing that internally for a long time, keeping me out of his life.

"You can go be with her," I heard myself say. "I'll be fine on my own, with the kids."

Ferr looked up at me. "I only met her eight months ago. I have nothing with her; she's just a friend. I still want my family." We stared at each other for a moment, and then I got up, walked into the bedroom, and closed the door.

The pain in my heart felt like it would burst out of me. I cried for days, wishing I could will myself to die at that moment. The loss, the emptiness was overwhelming. After sobbing in grief, I would yell at God. "Why? Why make me see all this... this mess? Why the suffering, God? You got me through cancer, but this is worse. What's the point of it all? I did everything right. I was patient. I worked hard, and now I'm the one suffering, for something that I didn't do! Tell me why, God??" I went through an endless loop of feeling worthless, hopeless, and in such grief and pain that nothing helped soften it. The love of my life was gone. I never truly knew just when he left my side. I never got to say goodbye to the man I had fallen in love with.

The true Ferr had come out and it terrified me. For so many years I'd been fooled – my family had been fooled. My strong foundation was now weak.

Concern for the kids drove me to continue. I knew that all the pressure was on me, on the only standing column. Everything would collapse on my innocent children. I had survived cancer only a year before, but this was far worse. There were doctors to help with external pain when I was battling cancer, but there was nothing for internal heartbreak.

I needed to refocus while I figured out what to do. I took my children and went to my mother's for a while. I needed her safety from further hurt, so that I could figure out how to salvage what was left. Unfortunately, during that stay I found out about another girl Ferr had been seeing during that same time frame as his original affair. Now the pain multiplied. I had thought I couldn't be hurt further, but I was wrong. If it was possible to die from heartbreak, I was convinced I would. This time, I knew who the other woman was – a young secretary, still a college student, who I met at a company party. More information emerged about the first woman as well. It turned out that Ferr had been with her for four years. Not two... and it was while I was pregnant with our son, Max. Four years! We are so naive to think that we can permanently hide the truth from others. Of course Ferr and the woman had agreed to lie about where they met. The truth always comes out.

Ferr and his lover had devised a plan, a story rehearsed in case they would get caught. When I learned that the story was false, I knew I hadn't been crazy for thinking that something was going on. All the evidence was there at all times. Somehow – because I trusted my own husband he made me believe that his brothers and employees did many of the suspicious things that bothered me. I saw women's shoes and earrings in his company car. Ferr told me that someone had planted them to destroy our marriage, same with the text messages.

In retrospect, it was all so clear. The belief that my beloved husband wouldn't lie was my greatest downfall.

Subconsciously, I must have known the truth, even then. I'd had a dream about the first lover he was seeing at that time and when I saw her in person, it was the same girl I saw in the dream. I had this dream several months before the truth came out. I remember telling him about it in the morning as he was dressing for the day and describing her to him. He said casually, "Don't worry, I would never do that." And he left for work. After I found out about the affair, all the pieces came together, it was a painful mess and I realized why it was that we could never communicate. He just had so much to hide.

Knowing that my children's future was in my hands, I decided to put aside my own pain and give Ferr a second chance. Surely, if we both worked at it, we could salvage a once-strong relationship. Maybe he just made a mistake and was really repentant. I hoped for the best.

Unfortunately, Ferr's "changes" were all a façade. He gave his lovers a new phone number to use and kept seeing them. In reality, Ferr was quite happy with his new life... and quite honestly, my trust in him had been so shattered that my heart wasn't in it. As we drove home from yet another fruitless counseling session, he sighed and said, "You don't know me, Ana. I'm not who you think I am."

"I know that now," I said in a low voice, as I gazed out the car window. My heart swelled with pain and the tears flooded my eyes. My throat tightened up, but I managed to speak, "You're not the person I married." From that point on, I was only Ana to him.

When we arrived home, I was calm and clear-eyed. Despite my incredible pain, I felt the peace of knowing I'd made a sound decision. I looked him in the eye. "I'm no longer going to waste my time or money on counselors. It takes two for this to work and you're not on the same page as I am. Continue to live your life the way you want. I have great values and I will not change them for you. I'm not willing to live a miserable life without love or respect. The kids and I will be just fine without you." Freed from the lies, my once-beloved husband moved out and never came back.

Ferr continued his relationship with the same two women, and a few others as well. He went on trips with different girls all the time, living the life he'd been living during the marriage but not bothering to hide it anymore. Everything was out in the open: buying properties, collecting cars, taking lavish vacations. In his mind, he was living a great life. Seeing all that affected me in my relationship with God. I always felt that I did all the right things and now I had to pay for something I didn't do. I saw no possible reason for all this pain. I needed support, and didn't know where to turn.

With my family in a distant city, I moved to different church for support, but I felt out of place all the time. After years with only a predetermined identity as a wife and mother, I was still trying to find myself as an individual. I was still a student, about to graduate from Interior Design and Photography school. Life felt awkward, difficult. I was busy with my kids, studying and going through a painful transition in my life. I missed my family sorely.

I quit attending church. Things were not going well for me after the divorce. I was struggling, heartbroken, and a long way from my family, isolated, and unsupported. A year after the divorce, things were still not going well for me. I had no direction and was lost in a fog of confusion, just going through the daily motions of what I needed to do to survive. Afraid of my own future, that was my lowest point in life.

Slowly, my confidence began to return. I realized that despite everything, I was going to be better than before. It was just a matter of time. I didn't know how to make it happen, yet I made the decision to leave fear behind and move forward. I recognized that God knew what He was doing with my life after all. Putting my faith in Him again was instrumental in my healing. I was getting stronger all on my own, but now I had support with God by my side. Through determination and a resolution to stay positive no matter what, I built my own business bit by bit, and now I can still be here for my teenage girls and my son. Hard work always pays off, and God faithfully gives you the strength to carry on each day. It took a long time for grief and healing, but I realized I couldn't move on in life without God. I trusted in Him, without reservation, and gave Him the control of what had been painfully out of control in my life. The results are well worth it.

*God's plan is to prosper you.*
*Jeremiah 29:11*

*"For I know the plans I have for you," declares the Lord,*
*"Plans to prosper you and not to harm you, plans to give*
*you hope and a future."*

When you allow God to take control of your life, things eventually work out for the best. Since the divorce, I've done so much. I met goals I never thought I could reach. Truly, I never knew who I was as an individual until I was by myself. The lesson I learned was, the grey and undeveloped areas of your life are opportunities for you to make your own path, wherever you want to go.

Grey is the midpoint between white and black and is the most flexible starting point to add color, to lighten or darken, to create. See grey areas with a different perspective, it's to your advantage. Make the best out of everything, for something good always comes out of bad. See it as an opportunity to move to the next step in your life. Learn and experience success. Know where you are going and what you want for your life.

Remember, life is short. Live each day like it is your last and plan your future as if you are going to be here forever. Make good choices so you have good memories to treasure. Always keep your foundation and values in place. Trust in God. The victory is always yours, for the past, no matter what it contains, can only prepare you for a better future. Love God, love yourself, and the rest will fall into place in its time.

I trusted in God and I can confidently say that He gave me all I needed to make it through, providing for me and my children at all times. These Bible verses comforted me during the worst of my journey.

To combat fear: Isaiah 41:10
*"Don't be afraid, because I am with you. Don't be intimidated; I am your God. I will strengthen you. I will help you. I will support you with my victorious right hand."*

God provides for you: Luke 12:24
*"Consider the ravens: they do not sow or reap, they have no storeroom or barn; yet God feeds them. And how much more valuable you are than birds!"*

What do you need? Matthew 7:7
*"Ask and it will be given to you; seek and you will find; knock and the door will be opened to you."*

**God never leaves you!** Despite the pain, within the darkness, He is always there to bring you a good future. He prospered me in every area in my life. Because of Him I am happy and at peace, and have more than enough. God is always there to bless you in abundance. Believe it and accept it.

**Precious stones are made beautiful because of the very difficult processes they go through. Diamonds require great pressure in their formation. Pearls happen when an irritant is transformed into something beautiful. Gold goes through fire in order to be purified. It's easy to forget the process and the difficulties that it takes to become such a desirable and beautiful jewel. It's the same with us. When we go through difficult times in our lives, we want to avoid the pain because we think that we're doing just fine as we are. But the pain and hardship can make us so much better! We need to trust that the bad situation we are in is a part of the formation process, to make a stronger and more beautiful jewel. Trust that the tough times will take us to our next best season, and a more beautiful creation of ourselves.**

# CHAPTER 3

# Losing a Part of Me

June 18, 2008. I'd been looking forward to this day for a long time: my last day of school at the university. I was about to accomplish one of my goals: a degree and soon, a career. Finishing my education was very important for me. My life as both a mother and a student was hard, monumentally challenging but very rewarding. I didn't sleep the night before my final exam. I was so excited that I was mentally and physically exhausted, but I couldn't possibly sleep. I prepared myself to turn in my final exam and to do my final presentation. I was ready to be done with everything. Days before I remember feeling sick, uncomfortable and anxious. I made my presentation, passed the final, and I felt a tremendous sense of relief.

Finally, I was done with school! I couldn't wait to walk the stage and receive my diploma. This is a special, transcendent moment for any student. I had finished all my requirements and reached the finish line. My adrenaline was still pumping from finishing such a momentous task.

Something unexpected happened the very next day. I had decided to go to the gym that morning to relieve the stress I was feeling. As I was working out, my sister Sole called me. I was so excited to hear from her. Sole is my next oldest sibling and we are very close. I told her about how excited I was about finally finishing school and how much I was looking forward to having that diploma in my hands. She interrupted me by saying, "Ana... go sit down. I have to talk to you."

My blood felt like it was draining from my body and my heart was pounding as I hurried to the locker room. I asked my sister, "What happened?"

Sole explained to me that our brother Mario was on his way to Mexico with his wife and family. She paused. "They had a car accident, Ana. And...the accident was really bad."

Mario and his family got ejected from their vehicle. My first thought was, *"Oh, no! My brother..."*

Sole continued. "They are in the hospital. Violet is badly injured and she needs surgery right away, Marie (their fifteen-year-old daughter) is okay and we are communicating through her. She broke her knee and needs surgery. Little Marc is fine, nothing happened to him."

I asked, "And my brother? How is he doing??" As tears came down my cheeks, I shook. She was not mentioning my brother. I asked her again, "Is he okay?" When Sole didn't answer, I asked again, crying, "Is he alive??" Inside I kept praying, *"Please, God... not my brother. He is very special to me, God! Please, please don't take him."*

Calmly, Sole said, "Our mother and brothers are on their way to the hospital in Chihuahua, Mexico. They're five hours away. I will call you back when I know more about Mario's condition. Marie says he is in surgery. We just don't know much about him yet. Don't worry, Ana. I'll call you when I know more."

Words can't describe the anxiety and frustration I felt. I was worried sick and far away from my family. I was already exhausted from school. Everything felt like a bad dream. I had to wait several hours before I had an answer about my brother's condition. Those hours were the longest of my life. I prayed for God to heal him, just how He healed me from cancer. "Nothing is impossible for You," I reminded Him. "Do it, please. I believe in miracles; make one in his life. Don't take my brother, please, God!" I was weeping, begging Him to not take Mario away from me. I had a special bond with this particular brother. I was going to see Mario in a week and we were going to celebrate my graduation with family. I wanted him to be there.

The next update was that our brother was badly injured but still alive. Doctors had to do emergency surgery on his head and he was in critical condition. I thought that if Mario was in surgery and was doing badly, at least he was still with us. That was better than hearing that he was gone forever.

I was seven hours away from my sister and my sister was five hours away from my brother. With all the confusion of getting updates through Marie and then from Sole, I just wanted to be there with him. I wanted to see him but I couldn't. I was hoping that he was still with us. I was feeling sad and hopeless and I couldn't do anything. I didn't know what the truth was but I just wanted to be next to him.

Then I got the call I never wanted to hear in my life. My sister told me that my mom and my two brothers had arrived at the hospital with Mario's family. Then she said, "We are getting everyone back to the United States today, but I have bad news." I heard Sole crying, heard her sad, low voice. "Mario didn't make it. He is gone."

"What happened?" I could hardly breathe. Sole clearly in shock, relayed what she had heard. "Violet told us that Mario was laying next to her. He asked her if she was okay and she said "yes." He closed his eyes, and he was gone. Those were his last words. My mom and brother saw him already. He died where the accident happened. They were not telling our niece Marie the truth about her dad until my other brothers arrived. My sister-in-law and niece need surgery right away so we are bringing them back. Our focus is on them right now. We are bringing them all to a hospital in El Paso. Our brothers are making arrangements to bring Mario back also as soon as possible."

I couldn't do anything for him anymore. No one could. I have never experienced such hopeless pain like I felt at that moment. My sister's words seemed unreal to me. My brother was gone and part of me was gone with him. When I finished talking to my sister, I cried and couldn't stop... it was hopeless. How could I make it past this pain?

I took the next flight back home to see my sister-in-law Violet and her children. When I walked into the hospital room, Violet was crying. She looked at me and in a weak voice said, "I'm so sorry that this happened. I just wanted Mario to meet my family. I didn't want this to happen to him."

Holding her hand, I told her, "Things happen. We don't have control of everything in life, but he will still be with us forever. Right now, we just want you to rest and get better." I was hurting, but I needed to be strong. We prayed with her for a quick recovery, both physical and emotional. Then I went to see my niece in a different room. It hurt me to see my niece in the hospital and to think that she had to continue her journey without her father. I had to be strong for her. I love her so much. We went out to see my ten-year-old nephew Marc in the waiting room. I gave him a hug and started talking to him, making sure he was okay. I wrapped my arms around him as family kept on coming to visit them.

My nephew Marc just wanted to give me details about the accident. "Aunt, I saw three bright lights and I just closed my eyes, then when I opened them, I was outside the truck, but nothing happened to me."

I said to him, "That was an angel. He was taking care of you."

"Yes, it was," he said.

Friends and family would walk in the hospital and my sweet young nephew would tell them the details of the accident and about the lights he saw. He is such a strong and brave boy. I closed my eyes and prayed for my brother's family, for speedy recoveries. They needed physical healing and healing from the trauma of losing their father.

Finally my brother's body arrived at the funeral home in town. I wanted to see my brother again, one more time. When the funeral home allowed us to go see him, I went with my siblings, my mother and Mario's son, little Marc.

My sister-in-law and niece couldn't leave the hospital yet. They were still recovering from surgeries. We spent days traveling back and forth between the hospital and the funeral home. It was a very dark time in my life. His wife and daughter wouldn't be discharged in time to attend the funeral. My heart grieved for them.

Violet wanted to go and see Mario one last time. We talked to the doctors and asked for permission to take her for a little bit, to say goodbye to her husband at the cemetery. We took full responsibility for her condition. She was still very bad off, restricted to a wheelchair, and in tremendous pain, but she went to say goodbye to her beloved husband on that hot summer day. I remember looking at her, my mother, and little Marc next to my brother's casket.

It was something I didn't want to remember. It had to be a bad dream. My mother and Violet were shaking from the unbearable pain. In a weakened state, Violet couldn't bear the wave of emotions. She fainted right next to my brother's casket. When she awoke she still refused to leave Mario's side. She was forced to say goodbye to her husband, the father of her two children. What a painful picture of life: a loved one in a casket, surrounded by sobbing friends and family.

One of the hardest things in life is to let a loved one go. When I said goodbye to my brother. I stood by the casket, weeping. *"Brother, tomorrow is my graduation. I wish you and I could be there together, celebrating. I know you would have been so proud of me. I want you to know that I love you.* I couldn't let him go. *"Mario, I am never going to forget you."* Hours passed as I stood beside him. I didn't want to, but I had to say goodbye. *I know you will forever be with me. Now you are in a better place. Take care of me, my angel!"* I didn't want to move from where his body was. I was not going to see his face ever again for the rest of my life.

At the cemetery, I was the last one to leave. I stayed there till they told me to leave his grave. Physically I was beyond exhausted, and losing my brother was too much for me. Back at my mother's house, I kept asking her, "How can we live without him?"

With tears in her eyes she said, "Ana, we need to accept it. That is the only way we can overcome this. We need to thank God for the years He allowed Mario to be with us."

*"But this is a lot of pain that I'm feeling…"*

I didn't get to attend my graduation. Instead of walking a stage, I was walking in a cemetery that day, to say goodbye forever to that very special person, my dear brother, the person I had such a special bond with. Mario was the life of all the family events. We shared so many years and special moments together, so many great memories from our childhood. Our bond became stronger when I was very sick with cancer. He was there for me at all times. He gave me comfort and strength. He treated me like a princess. I made sure to see Mario every time I visited my family in El Paso and other times he would visit me in San Antonio. He was like an angel on earth. I remember I told him I wanted a dog and he brought me one from El Paso. The dog was precious. It was a little Chihuahua named Paris. I believe Paris helped me heal faster after the chemotherapy treatments.

The last time I saw Mario was a month before he passed away. He hosted a party at his house that day in May, when I was visiting from San Antonio. We were celebrating my nephew's tenth birthday. Our last photograph was taken then. Who would have thought it would be the last time we would ever see each other?

I couldn't eat or sleep from the grief of missing Mario. There is a time for everything, and I was facing a time of emotional pain. In these times, we need God's guidance and comfort. I also learned to recognize the value of time. With God's help, time is what heals our pain. While we are here on earth, life is only our journey, not our destination. Time teaches you to recognize and accept your future just the way it is. I had to move on without that special person I had loved my entire life. Everything we go through in life is for a reason. I just couldn't see it then. As painful as it was, I needed to accept the future without him. I put my trust in God, and because of that I can still have a good journey. My brother finished his and I had to continue mine. Mario left me great memories. Therefore I thank God for giving me the privilege to have him as a brother and in my life for those years.

***Only time can heal the pain of grief and loss.***

Healing comes with time and acceptance, while keeping the memories alive but allowing time to soften and heal that pain. As you heal, it's important to have a positive attitude about your life, even your life without the one you love. Live in the present, not the past. Give yourself permission to live in the moment. Expect a great future with the people you love and who love you. Take one day at a time and be patient.

God never leaves our sides. He is our strength throughout each day. The experience can only make us stronger. This teaches us to treasure even more the time with our loved ones. We can use the tragic and uncontrollable to build us up.

It's been three years sense I lost my brother. I think about my wonderful brother Mario often. I know he is an angel in heaven and he is always with me. Time took care of that overwhelming pain, and transformed it into peace and great strength.

*Always trust in God:*
*Isaiah 41:13*

*"I, the Lord your God, hold your right hand and say to you,*
*Don't be afraid: I will help you."*

CHAPTER 4

# Single Life

I was married at sixteen and now at thirty-one, I found myself single again. Naive to the dating scene, I had no idea what I needed to do, how to start dating, or what kind of man to date after my divorce. There was such a huge difference with who I was now than who I was fifteen years earlier. I was no longer an innocent sixteen-year-old girl. Now I was a grown woman with three children. The world around me had changed too. I felt lost and confused. As a single woman I made new friends, similar in age, but most of them had never been married before and had no children. I found myself gravitating to people slightly older than myself, but I didn't fit in with that group either. In an effort to get my bearings, I took a step back and started to study people. I'd watch how they would act toward others in general and in relationships in particular. Meanwhile I continued with my education and my personal quest to find myself as an individual. My observations and studies of human nature were actually the best school for me to be able to understand how to embark on my new lifestyle.

To my surprise, dating was more difficult than what I expected. Games, sex, "friends with benefits," no commitment at all... it was all strange to me and I didn't understand any of it. I decided I would not put myself in a situation, or follow those same patterns. I didn't want to compromise my values. I would never get what I wanted if I went in this direction. knowing what I wanted in a relationship helped me to not settle.

As the saying goes, if you don't stand for something, you will fall for everything. It is almost impossible to find true happiness when you are in that situation. Moving all over the place without knowing where you are going next. That turns into "quantity" rather than "quality", and "quantity" only brings emptiness. There is no worthwhile relationship based on that.

Dating gave me an opportunity to examine what I knew about relationships and to guide my course with the right goals in mind. In life, you need to be selective and exclusive. Keep a sense of your own high value and quality as a person. It is similar to a brand-name product. If the product has saturated the market, is cheaply priced and making it available for everyone, but it loses its value. When the product is exclusive, it is more desirable and keeps its value. When you go to an exclusive brand's store, you go because you know of their quality and high standards. You are interested in buying their product exclusively. Once you find what you want, you pay the price and enjoy it. Quality is always more beautiful and appealing. It is the same with relationships.

**If someone is not willing to invest time in you, it is because that person is not interested. This does not mean that you are less valuable. It simply means that this is not the right person for you.**

Sooner or later the right person will cross your path. It's important to have similar foundations. There is a greater change to make it a success. know what you are getting yourself into before you let someone in your life. Dating is the first step to knowing someone. This is the time to build a friendship with the other person. Everything worthwhile is built in steps, one at a time. This is true for relationships as well. Relationships are built over time, in steps creating a firm structure. When we move to fast we create a weak foundation. That relationship might collapse as quick as it was built. Self-control is what we use during the dating stage to avoid mistakes and undesirable issues.

In most dating scenarios, men often want to skip steps, and women mistake that eagerness with love and a meaningful relationship. Physical intimacy should not be considered in early dating stages. You don't know each other well. It is better to wait until you both have a commitment. When the commitment comes, that means you know each other better, have chemistry, and share similar interests and direction in your life.

Another important tool in dating is to be able to read body language. Body language says a lot about a person, showing a person's wants, intentions, and personality. Many mistakes can be avoided if we can read what the body is communicating. At times body language will be able to tell us more than the person is really telling us with words. Being able to "read" people this way is a skill you'll use in all areas of your life, and is well worth paying attention to.

I went on several dates where the first thing the man would talk about was his material wealth. In my mind I couldn't help wondering if they were trying to sell themselves to me based on what they have, rather than who they were as an individual. It's not good when you start talking about what we can offer or what we have to impress the other person. If we have a lot to offer in a relationship, it will show by our conduct and behavior . It doesn't need to be stated from the outset or in every conversation. Usually people tell you what they have or who they are to distract you from what they don't have. They do it out of insecurity. This tactic is fine for advertising commercials but backfires in relationships. After all, a good product virtually sells itself. Always be you.

Most of us want to achieve our goals and feel fulfilled. One common mistake we make in relationships, we make it our foundation. Love is free and we have to respect that, the partner can only be a compliment to your life. Otherwise, if that relationship fails, we will feel like a failure. By Staying confident of who we are, gives us a high value. Never spend all your energy looking for love; you will get tired and never find it. Focus on yourself as an individual. Enjoy your own journey of self-improvement and accomplishing personal goals.

We all have a **purpose** and a **mission.** *You are here because God decided to give you the gift of life. What are you most passionate about? That's your mission.* It makes us feel accomplished when we find it and apply it in our daily lives. Each of us possesses talents and we need to use them to bless others. We are here to help each other without expecting an earthly reward. ***God gave us special gifts to help us with in life. Some of them are:*** *prophesy, serve, teach, encourage, lead, show mercy,* and *giving. Romans 12: 6-8*

When I discovered my gifts in my life everything made perfect sense.

I came to the conclusion that **God** was the only foundation that could keep me secure and hold me together, just like a real foundation keeps a building strong and stable.

In my journey I discovered my strengths and weakness. Using my strengths to help me work on my weaknesses, helped me to build myself as an individual. I also discovered what I like and don't like, whether in lifestyles or in relationships with people, so that I could make wise choices in the future. I worked on the image that I wanted to portray, through what I wear and the look I wanted for myself base on my personality, resulting in Self-confidence. Fundamentally, I took the time to evaluate where I was standing and where I was going in life. I set short-term and long-term goals and through the process I found my true identity.

Along the way, I found the true value of **"love"** and **"time"**. They both bring such peace when you recognize the depth of them.

*Love is what gives life meaning. Everything you need has its perfect timing.*

I learned to be patient and never put my full focus on only that one need in my life. It took me about two years to heal after my divorce, dissolving our 15 year marriage. I wanted to feel the love I felt as a young teen once again. But I realized that it was not the time for me to be in a relationship. That was out of my control. Why focus so much on only that area of my life when I can improve in other areas over which I truly do have control? The right love relationship can only be fulfilled in its own time. There is a time for everything, and I realized that this was the time for me to grow as an individual and fulfill my dreams.

By putting my focus on things which I could control, I accomplished many goals and kept myself happily occupied. I made changes to grow in my profession and improve my personal life and my children's lives. I found myself single but not available, and I was very happy. I had so much to do that a relationship was not on my mind anymore. My priority was to find myself as a whole, to feel complete. I didn't want to depend on someone else to fulfill that area of my life, nor think that my happiness had to come from another individual.

I have the key to my own happiness. Now I feel complete and satisfied. I learned that a relationship is only a complement to my life, not its total focus. If a relationship were to happen, I would welcome it but I was fine without it. Now I am educated, fulfilled in so many areas, and I finally feel complete.

**Wait for what you want,** and keep your sense of your own value. Never settle. Settling for quantity over quality only puts your own standard and values down. Quantity is just so easy to get. Quality takes more work, but we have a better opportunity of making it last.

**"Dating"** is the time to learn about someone you like. It works well when you build a friendship first, without being intimate. Sometimes chemistry or physical attraction is there, and when it is, that's when you use self-control. What happens if you are intimate while dating? This will affect the relationship in the future. Sex is an act meant for after you both have a commitment. A commitment is made when you both know each other well and agree to work toward the same outcome for the relationship. This is done in a verbal conversation; do not assume something that is not. At times we try to go the "express way" to get what we want, and the relationship fails because we try to fulfill that need too fast.

## How much information do you share on your first date?

Personal information is like your valuables. Don't give them to a stranger you don't know anything about. Before you meet your date, know what you are willing to share. It should be only basic information, nothing too personal. Be polite when you get asked a personal question, but if you think it is too soon to share, you can say that you will share that information later. As the relationship progresses, you can be more personal. In life everything good has structure, designed by steps. Nature and people are a perfect example of this fact. We do everything in steps. Relationships are formed the same way.

### Relationships are almost like a bank account.

You open an account in the bank of your preference. Then you make a small deposit. We never deposit all that we have into a bank that we don't know anything about. Once you know that bank and have some history with them, you give and take, deposits and withdrawals. It's the same with dating. As the relationship develops, give-and-take is required on both sides to make it a success. Eventually you build a solid relationship.

### Be aware and avoid getting hurt.

Always listen to your inner voice. If something looks and sounds wrong, it's because it is wrong. When it is right, everything is clear, with no confusion about it. Stay in healthy relationships and be selective. Never compromise your values to keep a weak relationship only because you need someone in your life. Stand up for yourself and let the other person know what is acceptable and what is not.

### We live in a world with many single women and men.

Some people don't know who they are or what they want. Others say there are too many options, so why settle for one? When the relationship starts wrong, it ends wrong. A relationship that was not built the right way collapses in the future. Others think that it is too hard to maintain a relationship, so they don't even try to invest time in it. They carelessly let it go, moving from person to person, finding emptiness everywhere and never achieving what they really want. What is good for you is never easy, and you can't value something that is given to you casually. You will value it if it costs you time, effort, and money.

### By nature, human beings are hunters and thrive on challenges.

If something costs you time and effort, you will value and take care of it. That's what a relationship is meant to be. If you don't value a relationship, it is because it didn't cost you anything to get it.

When a hunter goes out hunting, he knows why he is there and that it is going to take effort, but it will be a fun experience. He prepares for the hunt. It takes time and patience, and finally after many hours or even days he makes the kill. He feels the joy and pride of his accomplishment. Now imagine two animals by his front door: the one he killed, and one that just appeared out of nowhere, lying dead at his doorstep. They are both the same size and breed of animal. Which one is he going to value more? The one he killed himself. He invested time in that one. The other dead animal by his door has no value to him. He has no connection with that other one. Only the one he killed will be valued and become a prize on his wall.

We can't value someone we don't know or we haven't invested time in. Sometimes you are just not interested in getting to know the other person. Don't be so desperate to get what you want if the other person doesn't show the same interest. What you are doing is lowering your value. The other person will never value you. Never be desperate. You don't have to throw yourself at the other individual. That will be a turn-off for the other person. Give it some time. If the relationship you wanted doesn't happen, it was not meant to be. There is someone better for you, but you have to wait for its time.

### Being friends is important in any love relationship.

*A friend is there for you and cares about you at all times (Proverbs 17:17 – "A friend loves at all times.")*

If you've found someone who intrigues you, the first step is the friendship. Everything starts from the bottom up. When you are building a business, you get information about the business to see if it's what you really want. There is always preparation you need to do. It might entail lots of research, taking classes, or doing whatever is necessary to fully prepare. Then you take action. When you gather all the pieces of information, you become passionate and make your new business a mission. Once your business is underway, you start to invest time and money. Investing time and money is how the business will grow. Along the way you will reap the rewards of your investment. That's how relationships work also. Relationships are an amazing gift from God. Never lose the true meaning of it. Develop a relationship wisely, from the bottom up, and you'll enjoy the reward of a solid, loving partnership with someone you truly like and respect.

## *Make decisions based on what you want in a relationship.*

I based my decisions on my values and what I wanted in a relationship. I found happiness with my decisions. If it is not the time, it's not the time. Remain calm and enjoy your life. That shows a confident person, and that is very attractive.

I had the opportunity to do some research on people of different age groups, and this is the list of what they shared.

## *Desirable qualities in a person:*

- Confidence, knowing what you want in life, taking care of your appearance, being clean, kind, and a positive attitude.

## *Undesirable qualities in a person:*

- Being sloppy, clingy, needy, or desperate. Negativity, insecurity, cockiness, and emptiness. Being conceited, shallow, or pretending to be someone they are not.

## *What do men want?*

1. Love and a friend who is attractive in some way, with common interests

2. Respect

3. Someone who gives him his space

4. Sex is an important factor

5. A confident woman

6. A woman who is focused on her life

7. Romance

8. A nice girl in public a woman who can be honest, be herself, and be loyal to him

## *What do women want?*

1. Love, a friend, someone attractive in some way, with common interests

2. Confident man

3. A man who knows what he wants in life

4. Romance

5. Understanding

6. A man who gives her space

7. Sex

8. A man who makes her feel loved and special a man
   who can be honest, be himself and loyal to her

*A confident man or woman is always more attractive than
someone who is insecure. Overall, we all look for similar
qualities in each other.*

### Why can't I find what I am looking for in a relationship?

- Do you know what you want?

- Do you believe in yourself?

- Are you scared that if you get what you want, you'll need to leave many things behind?

- Are you afraid of making mistakes?

- Are you making the same mistakes over and over?

- Are you afraid to get hurt?

*Relationships are a gamble if we don't play, we will never have an opportunity to win. Everyone wants to be successful in relationships. If we don't take risks, we will never experience the wonders of a relationship.*

### Do you feel that you are missing something in your life?

Sometimes it's good to be alone and examine your life. Take an inventory. See what we have and what we need, what is good and what is not. When we stand back, we always see life from a different perspective. Connect with nature. Take a walk while looking at an endless ocean. look at the sky full of stars. It is an inspiration to look at God's creation. How amazing to see all the beautiful things He has created for us to enjoy. His creation gives us a sense of peace and calmness, inspiring us to move forward in our life with a positive attitude.

He created so many beautiful things. I feel so small when I look at His majestic works of art, the heavens and the earth. I always find peace and take a new direction or reinforce what I am doing to better myself. We are created with a body, mind and soul, fulfilling ourselves in all three areas creates balance. When we feel fulfilled, we are better with relationships. To fulfill those individual needs of body, mind, and soul daily. These are some of the things I found interesting.

1. **The Body:** Work out, go for a walk, dance, swim, get into sports and stay active for both your physical and mental health.

2. **The Mind:** Study a subject you are interested in or that will improve our quality of life. Sing, listen to inspirational music (relaxing or calming music), paint a work of art, be creative, read books, write, connect with God through nature, take vacations to interesting places, protect your mind from thoughts that can harm your body and soul and disturb your peace.

3. **The Spirit:** Connect with God, have a relationship with Him. Make God the foundation of you life. Allow God to guide you. Be grateful and acknowledge that He is God. Without Him we

cannot feel fulfilled, happy, or successful. Without God, we will always feel a void, even when you have material wealth.

*When we find balance in these three areas, we feel fulfilled as individuals.*

## Different phases in life:

The single life is a beautiful stage of life. There is so much we can do. Fulfill personal goals. It's easier to create personal balance. We experience freedom in different ways. This is the time to grow as individuals.

### *Dating*

We start dating because we seek a connection. During the dating stages we will know when we find the perfect match. Dating can sometimes be challenging, have patience. Trust your instinct, you'll know what's right for you.

### *Friendship*

Friendship is creating a bond with a person you know and invested your time with. Women should always set clear boundaries with their male friends. When sex is involved in what is otherwise a friendship, it creates confusion. Keep the friendship within its original meaning and enjoy the blessing of that. Avoid the painful issues and mistakes that happen when you share intimacy with a friend, we have a better chance on making a good friend, best friend or a committed relationship.

## *Exclusive relationship*

Chemistry is an important factor, however common interests, love, respect, and mutual agreement on the direction of the relationship are vital. Valuable time has been invested to get to this point. By this time you will know if marriage will be a part of this relationship.

## *Marriage*

Marriage comes in its own time. When you both are on the same page, things feel natural after time has being invested in each other's lives. You both will feel a mutual need of being with each other, taking the relationship into a marriage.

Marriage is a covenant and there are many blessings when you honor and respect the pact of marriage. Fidelity and communication are your foundation for a successful marriage and will bond you to one another. Loving and cherishing one another makes the relationship grow.

## Sex

Sex was created for reproducing and to develop a bond with the person we are committed to. While dating you create a basis for this bond. Compromising this can only lead to confusion and emotional pain. It can create a weak relationship.

If we know that something isn't good for us, why invest our time in it? We all know what is right. Living only for that moment will affect us. In time we will know whether the person who we're with is the right person for us.

There are blessings that were created for us to experience in the proper time. Always doing what is best for us long-term. No one can make us do something we don't want to do. Making good choice for a successful future, we will find fulfillment and happiness with in.

We see so much emptiness in people's lives, so much confusion, broken hearts, depression, financial troubles, emotional pain and an entire host of other issues. The question is, "Why?" Could casual sex be the cause of some of the issues? These could be effects of using sex for selfish reasons. Sex is a powerful and precious gift that was given to us by God, but if we misuse it, it can cause us confusion and bring unpleasant issues.

*To everything there is a season, and a time to every purpose under the heaven. (Ecclesiastes 3:1)*

CHAPTER 5

# Sex and Relationships

We all want to experience sex within a loving, committed relationship. Here are some truths to guide us in our journey.

Can a man love you if he doesn't know you well? The only way he can develop feelings for you is with time. Sex needs to wait. Postponing it creates a tension, but if he really likes you, he will stick around. That's how you start a foundation for a relationship and love. By understanding the nature of men and women, we can make better choices.

When we have sex, we share our whole being with the other person. In the wrong circumstances, that might bring unpleasant issues. Waiting until there is a commitment, until marriage, is a better choice for you. Every good thing takes time and if both take the time to build it, will be harder to dissolve. Marriage comes with many blessings from God.

Casual sex blocks those blessings and brings on confusion, heartache, and emptiness.

This information will help you understand how we were created. By understanding how God made men and women, we can make better choices and experience greater blessings in our lives.

Men were created to spread their seed and reproduce by having many choices. This is the reason why men always think about sex. Some are open about it, others are not, but sex is in the mind of a man. Their high levels of testosterone place a constant pressure on them to experience it frequently. Sex for men is only a physical act that eases the urge of the pressure when they are not in a committed relationship. This is why some men disappear after they get what they want casually. They can move on and find it elsewhere. This kind of sex was to fulfill a physical need, not an act of love.

Women seek quality and love. Women were created to seek as many admirers as they can to make the best choice for a good seed. Women's testosterone levels are lower, which is why women are concerned first with love rather than with sex. Love is the proof that a woman needs a man to assure her that he will stay to help with the upbringing of that fruit. For a woman, sex is an emotional connection. That is why women need to be selective and exclusive.

Oxytocin is a hormone found in men and women. This hormone is released during sex. It is known to increase levels of trust and makes you feel connected with the other person. *This is why we feel a connection after intimacy.*

If there is no commitment means no exclusiveness, and don't expect a good outcome from casual sex.

After a man is intimate with a woman, he usually disconnects from the person. This is the same person who was previously saying he cares about you. He may disappear for days or weeks because he needs to regain the feeling of independence. The oxytocin hormone released during sex makes a man feel dependent.

When there is a commitment and exclusiveness, he cares more about you. That's how God created us if you are intimate, you become one. There is a blessing from God when you wait. Casual sex with no commitment creates confusion and can destroy a potential relationship. We were not created to have casual sex, which is why we see unhealthy relationships, confusion, broken hearts, and many sexually-transmitted diseases that can harm the body, mind and spirit.

When we have casual sex, we risk many blessings. One of those blessings is our sense of self-worth. Great values and qualities create: beauty, confidence, and a high self-esteem. If you are not exclusive this can affect our self-esteem as part of the effect. Sharing ourselves with so many people can affect other potential love relationships as well because of unwanted experiences and memories. We not only share a moment and the body but the spirit is also a part of the overall act.

Have boundaries and don't let anyone invade your personal territory. Stay away from those who don't respect your boundaries and decisions.

Sex was created to be a quality experience and to be exclusive. "Intimacy" is defined as something very personal and private. When the other person is interested in getting to know you for a potential love relationship, any sex that occurs before you get to know each other well might create a weak relationship. Always base a love relationship on God and follow His guidelines we will have better chances to make it a success.

**God gave us self-control to use when necessary, to help you achieve a happier future.**

Self-control is like a filter to our life, allowing only what is good for us, and rejecting the bad. When we don't use it, we allow everything to come to us with no evaluation and no boundaries. The result creates instability: physically, mentally, emotionally, and spiritually.

## *How can I be a better judge of character?*
## *How can I make better choices?*

Know who you are and what you want. Things happen in their own time and can't be rushed or forced. If you are always looking for "the one", you will look desperate. Take the time to find out more about a person you might be interested in. This process takes time, so don't rush it. Evaluate their image, how they portray themselves.

How an individual dresses, talks, and treats you, says a lot about their life and who they are inside. Who their friends are says a lot about him or her, as do their hobbies and interests. Make sure he or she is single. Never, ever assume anything. Always ask for clarification to prevent future issues. First build a friendship while keeping sex out of the equation, and invest time in a relationship. Make sure you have things in common. If both of you are on the same page, this is a good sign.

**When you meet the right person, things will feel right. Do not ever ignore this simple truth. If you have to question something, that's a red flag.**

Pay attention to it. When someone is truly interested in you, they'll be sure to make the relationship happen – if they don't, they're not interested in a relationship, no matter what they say. Remember, actions speak louder than words. Don't waste your time if you feel you have invested in the relationship and the other person has not. Let it go. That person was not for you. Always, always think positive. The right person will show up when you least expect it.

**Always ask God to guide you in whatever decision you make, and don't ignore the counsel of wise friends who know you well.**

God gave us free will to make our own choices. His plan is for us to prosper, but we need to live in obedience. We all know what is right. **Listen to your intuition.** Our minds will give us signs of what is not healthy for our spirit. We want something new and fresh for our lives, but we go in circles creating the same unsuccessful ways to try to reach our goals and desires. Making changes is the only way we can see new beginnings in future relationships. Keep your **self-respect** and **maintain your boundaries.** Trust that if you follow the structure of relationships, you will experience your heart's desire. *(Psalms 37:5 (NIV))*

# Epilogue

Whenever we feel insignificant or afraid to face the obstacles in our life, remember that all things serve a purpose that will benefit us at the end. The situation we're facing now will teach us a lesson, make us stronger or prepare us for the next event in our life. I look back on my own life and without all the events I've shared with you, I would never have come to fully experience God's power in the amazing ways that I did.

Many times I did not understand why I had to face such crises. I felt I was inadequate to deal with such situations. But with time, everything comes together for good. Now I see that all the events of my life, both good and bad, were steps in my journey to get me to where I needed to be. I was able to discover what I had and what I was made of. I learned, through many experiences, that God created us well, and equipped us to be survivors and experience tremendous victories on earth. My life underwent some drastic changes, and as a result I am happier and stronger now than I could have possibly imagined.

An event always has a purpose and a goal, a beginning and an end. Sometimes we are happy, while at other times we are definitely not. Chaotic times have a purpose too.

Always look for good in all situations. Intense events make you experience the full range of your emotions and they let you know you're alive. I am reminded of the four seasons we have in the year, they all have a purpose and a specific time. The seasons come and go; the cold season brings death and the beautiful sunny weather nurtures new life. Good comes from each and every one of the seasons and all are necessary. There are times for healing, and times for growth. Whatever season you are in; make the very best out of it. There is something good in it for you. The victory is always there for you to take. Don't let it go. *(Romans 8:37)*

Always move forward and never look back. Look forward to an exciting future. A good attitude changes things around for the best. I witnessed and experienced some great victories at a very young age. Those events changed my life and now I have a profound happiness. At times I thought I wouldn't survive. Now I am living a joyful life because of my trust in God. He led me through those tough times. There is always a lesson to learn. Grow, share, and support those who need to hear about your victories.

Treat surviving an experience as a personal victory in life. If you are facing a tough time, stay strong and determined. Nothing is really fruitless. Remain calm, keep a positive attitude, and be determined to find the good in the bad. Life is easier if you take one day at a time, enjoying the blessings of each precious day. Be patient and time will bring the victory. A better future is waiting for you, filled with blessings, victories, and moments of peace.

*Psalm 46:10 –*
*"Keep calm and know that I am God."*

*Jeremiah 29:11 -*
*"For I know the plans I have for you," declares the Lord,*
*"plans to prosper you and not to harm you, plans to give you*
*hope and a future."*

*Isaiah 41:10 -*
*"Don't be afraid, because I am with you. Don't be*
*intimidated; I am your God. I will strengthen you. I will*
*help you. I will support you with my victorious right hand."*

*Philippians 4:13 -*
*" I can do all things through Christ who strengthens me."*

Enjoy your journey! Make happiness your best friend and pursue your purpose and mission. Evaluate what you want and what you are looking for and embrace being you. We were each born with our own identity. That is what makes us different from everyone else. We are precious and priceless.

We are greater than our bad situations. God equipped us to survive and to deal with hardships that come our way. We all get inspired by certain persons, and in the same way, we inspire others. That fact that we are here has its reason and purpose.

*(Be strong and Courageous.. Joshua 1:9)*

*(I am with you always.. Matthew 28:20)*

# *About the Author*

Ana was born in Zacatecas, Mexico. At the age of ten, she and her family moved to El Paso, Texas. Ana credits her mother with giving her great values and a good foundation, to always believe in God. At the tender age of 16, she married. Ana moved to San Antonio, Texas and completed her education in the fields of Interior Design, Photography and Fashion.

In 2004, Ana battled cancer. Her victory over cancer was a transition that would forever change her life and her outlook on how to live. 2006 brought more changes, as she found herself facing life on her own after fifteen years of marriage and a painful divorce. Yet her new singlehood enabled her to find her own purpose in life and to clarify what she wanted in her relationships. Ana's closest brother passed away in a tragic accident in 2008 – an incident that made her value family even more. Throughout all the struggles, Ana would tell herself,

"This out-of-control event has to have a reason... I just have to stay strong and let God take control." She saw these situations as opportunities for growth.

Ana has learned firsthand that the bad events in her life have helped shape her into the person she always dreamed of becoming. After Ana's victory over cancer, she only wanted to forget her struggles and avoid reliving her painful past. Yet Ana would find herself sharing her testimony with people she encountered in daily life who needed a message of hope. After yet another vivid dream about writing a book, Ana felt compelled to put her experiences down on paper.

*Writing "Staying in Control" was part of Ana's new purpose. She has found tremendous joy in helping others in their struggles. Ana says, "I'm just a messenger. I want everyone to know that there is hope and that anyone can achieve the successful life they long for. Stay in control of your own life and when things are out of your control, give it all to God. Trust and believe that everything will work out for the best. Always proclaim your victory. Through my faith, my life was transformed forever." Ana hopes that in these pages, you'll find the inspiration to transform your own life, with the help of a loving God.*

-Lisa Moon

www.anamariesilva.com

*A joyful heart is good medicine, but a crushed spirit dries up the bones. Proverbs 17:22, (esv)*

Reflections: